FADING ADS OF GLOUCESTER

CHRIS WEST

The History Press

In memory of Terry West

First published 2014

The History Press
The Mill, Brimscombe Port
Stroud, Gloucestershire, GL5 2QG
www.thehistorypress.co.uk

British Library Cataloguing in Publication Data.
A catalogue record for this book is available from the British Library.

ISBN 978 0 7524 9265 0

Typesetting and origination by The History Press
Printed in India

CONTENTS

FOREWORD

Painted signs have a long history, dating at least as far back as Roman times where the remains of political slogans and advertising for brothels adorned the walls of Pompeii and Herculaneum. While Gloucester's fading ads don't share the city's own Roman origins, they are surprisingly numerous given its relatively small size. Nearby Bath shares a similarly high number, although this is partly explained by the restrictions placed on the development of listed buildings there.

These fading ads, or ghostsigns as they are sometimes known, once used walls and paint to promote the wares of local and national businesses. In some cases, retailers and manufacturers would advertise side by side to benefit from the respective goodwill that they could offer each other. This type of 'privilege' advertising was used widely by flour producers, notably Hovis, and so it is no surprise to find a Hovis sign alongside the painted advertisement for Sparkes Bakery on Ryecroft Street.

Behind every sign is a story and in this book's travels through Gloucester we learn about some of the characters that once dominated the city's commercial landscape. Many of these have long since ceased trading but the remains of their advertising, coupled with Chris West's research, brings their lives back into focus. These stories vary from the rise and fall of the local bottling firm, Talbot's, to one member of the Lea family who took four different women, all called Mary, to be his wife.

The fading ads featured in this book will continue to weather and fall victim to urban renewal. Nonetheless, they capture the essence of how advertising and signage was once routinely hand-crafted by skilled signwriters, as opposed to the identikit streets that dominate today. I would urge getting out and seeing them while they are still here and, while doing so, imagine what life was like when Messrs Hamblin, Lane and Reynolds once touted their wares from the walls of the city.

Sam Roberts, 2014

Sam Roberts writes the Ghostsigns blog at www.ghostsigns.co.uk and, in 2010, curated the History of Advertising Trust Ghostsigns Archive. He has made numerous contributions to books, journals and magazines on the topic of hand-painted signs and has a soft spot for those found in Cambodia.

ACKNOWLEDGEMENTS

I would like to thank the following: commissioning editor Matilda Richards for supporting this book from the start; Jane West, Simon West and Emily Allsopp for their help checking over the text; Jill West for sharing her memories; Gill and Tony Hart for introducing me to the Gloucestershire Archives; the helpful staff at Gloucestershire Archives, particularly Paul Evans for his help via the Barton and Tredworth Community Heritage website; Jacqueline Rees Adams, Robert Sandford and Theresa Farragher-Steward for their help in tracking down some of the more elusive historical facts; and Lucy Simpkin, Juanita Hall and Chris Ogle for their work on editing and proofing the text.

All modern photographs © Chris West, and all other images from the author's collection, with the following exceptions:

P34: Talbot's Bottle, courtesy of cob-1888.
P60: Robert Opie Collection at Albert Warehouse, courtesy of Darrel Kirby.

The cover and internal design are also by Chris West.

ABOUT THE AUTHOR

Chris West is a graphic designer born in Gloucester. He has a fascination with vintage advertising and graphics, and enjoys discovering old signs and advertising, particularly in his home city.

INTRODUCTION

It's become something of a cliché to say that history is all around us. Usually this refers to the obvious – cathedrals, churches, Tudor houses and castle ruins – but there are more subtle yet equally important pieces of our past dotted around every town and city in the country. I am of course referring to the old signs and adverts that can be seen in faded paintwork on brick walls, chiselled stone, or in rusting ironwork atop gates and fencing. Most towns have one or two famous old signs that everyone knows, but you would be surprised how many others are hidden away, or simply overlooked. I have discovered fantastic signs in places you'd never expect; up on the rooftops or partially obscured by modern signage, some of which I had walked past hundreds of times before without ever noticing.

There is an intrigue and a charm to the old hand-painted signs, each possessing the unique personal touch of the sign painter. There are slight imperfections and little flourishes of individualistic flair that make modern vinyl lettering and cheaply produced signs look rather soulless. The growing interest in these old signs and traditional hand-production methods could reflect the beginning of a cultural shift regarding signage and branding. People are becoming disillusioned with mass production and the rushed creation of utilitarian signs that often lack character. Logo designs are all expected to be 'slick' and 'professional' these days, a look which, although perfectly reasonable for a bank or a solicitors to desire, is perhaps less appropriate for a small café or bookshop. Whilst large companies usually have very successful branding, smaller businesses are often forced to try and achieve the same on the cheap – this can often result in self-designed signage with, let's say, mixed results. A part of my soul dies every time I see a promise of professionalism displayed proudly in Comic Sans or a plumber's services advertised on the side of a van in a curiously medieval font.

There is no sense in pointing the finger in any particular direction, be it at designers, business owners or consumers, but the undeniable truth is that our high streets are losing their individuality. Where towns once offered completely different businesses and services to one another, many of our high streets are now becoming almost indistinguishable, as nine out of ten shops are the same chains seen everywhere. There are many complex reasons for this – the modern ease of mass-produced signage; the juggernaut-like multinationals, whose expansion seems endlessly exponential; the pressures on small businesses in the current economic climate; the pull of a known brand on consumers, be it conscious or subconscious, logical or emotional.

Looking at a number of these old signs and adverts may be a nostalgia trip for some, but even if they have been around long before you took your first breath, I hope that there is still much to admire about them – the craftsmanship, the character and the differing styles of old, not least their knack for survival after all these years!

Should you uncover any old signs not featured in this book please get in touch – I would love to see them!

Chris West, 2014

I

CITY CENTRE

The Wessex Hotel

Market Parade/Clarence Street

The Wessex Hotel was built in 1903 and featured twenty-three bedrooms to serve overnight travellers from Gloucester's railway stations, of which there were two at the time. The painted sign above the rooftops has faded considerably and the manicule that points the way to the hotel is now

barely recognisable. However, the name above the door is still very clear, standing out in brilliant white amongst the green, glazed tiles of the ground-floor façade. On the other doorway is a sign reading 'Wessex House', a later name for the building. The Wessex name refers to the Kingdom of Wessex, an Anglo-Saxon kingdom in south-west England, which lasted from roughly the sixth century to the tenth. The hotel closed around 1945 and has since housed offices and the Namaste Indian restaurant. Although the ground floor is currently lying empty, hopefully a new purpose will be quickly found for this charming building.

WESSEX HOUSE

1895
THE
HOTEL

The Regal

St Aldate Street/King's Square

Work began on building the Regal cinema in 1939 but it was not completed until 1956, due to the outbreak of the Second World War. The cinema went through multiple incarnations – it became the ABC in 1963, and then Cannon in 1988, before closing for the final time in 1990. The Beatles made their only appearance in Gloucester here, when they played on 18 March 1963, although they weren't top of the bill! Their set list was as follows: 'Love Me Do', 'Misery', 'A Taste Of Honey', 'Do You Want To Know A Secret', 'Please Please Me' and 'I Saw Her Standing There'. In 1996 it became The Regal, a Wetherspoons pub, which is still open today. It features some rather obvious nods to the building's cinematic past inside, including a large model of King Kong, a cityscape backdrop, suspended model aeroplanes and Oscar-style figures guarding the staircase. It is refreshing to see a piece of Gloucester's history remembered in this way.

AL

WETHE

Lea & Co. Furnishers

St Aldate Street/Northgate Street

Lea & Co. were well-established house furnishers and antique dealers, whose premises once took up practically the entire length of St Aldate Street. One 1887 advert claimed that Lea & Co. were the answer to 'how to furnish for 20 guineas', including a 'kitchen, two bedrooms, sitting-room and dining-room, or an eight-roomed house for 90 guineas.' There were two very interesting characters in the Lea family, both named John. The seventeenth-century John Lea married four wives, all called Mary, whilst the eighteenth-century John Lea is said to have been one of the developers of Pitman Shorthand – a phonetic shorthand system. The company was well-regarded within the city, and even did work at the Kingsholm rugby stadium in 1954, laying lino in the

kitchen at a price of 8 guineas. The company briefly became Pickford Lea & Co. in the 1960s, before closing down a few years later. As you can see, there are still three instances of the Lea & Co. name visible above the rooftops: two painted signs and one stone engraving.

... A ...

St Aldate Street

All that remains of this curious sign is a single letter 'A', and a few partial remnants of other letters from what appears to be two different signs. It is anyone's guess what it was for ... perhaps a St Aldate Street business, or maybe even an advert for a film being shown at the Regal?

E.C. Johnstone

Hare Lane

This empty building was most recently home to Wyedean Wholefoods, an organic food shop. However, the removal of their sign has revealed the very faint trace of an older sign on the board behind – that of the photographer E.C. Johnstone, who sold photography equipment and art supplies from around 1961 to 1980.

The Imperial Inn

Northgate Street

This elaborately decorated Grade II listed inn is a wonderful example of Victorian architecture, with its glazed green tiles, etched windows and intricate crest above the doorway. The attractive sign is made up of ornate tiling. The building dates back to approximately 1890, although the pub itself is much older. It was first recorded as a beerhouse in 1722 and was called The Plough. The name was changed to The Imperial around 1877 following a new lease to a George Cummings. The current owners have thankfully resisted the temptation to modernise the frontage in any way, although as you might be able to see the original sign has been rather perplexingly covered by a SkySports banner. I was lucky enough to turn up on a windy day, however, and catch this shot with it blowing up in the air.

New Inn

Northgate Street

The name is somewhat ironic, as the New Inn is in fact the oldest pub in Gloucester, having been built not long before 1455 to house pilgrims visiting the shrine of Edward II at nearby Gloucester Cathedral. At the time of completion it was said to be the largest inn in the country, capable of accommodating over 200 guests (mainly in dormitory-type rooms). It is said to be the most complete surviving example of a medieval courtyard inn with galleries in Britain. One eighteenth-century landlord, Mr Nelson, was renowned for bringing bizarre shows and spectacles to the inn. Among the spectacles he offered for just *6d* were Maria Theresa, the 2ft 10in Corsican Fairy, life-sized waxwork models of the Royal Family, a mermaid captured off the Mexican coast, and wild animal shows featuring leopards, lions, tigers, hyenas and llamas. Charles Rolls, co-founder of Rolls-Royce, once had a rather unfortunate stay here in December 1896, after the brakes had failed on his Peugeot car on the steepest section of Birdlip Hill, causing him to career downhill at great speed. In the morning he repaired the brakes only to suffer another mishap: he had left the car in gear, so when he swung the starting handle on the front of the vehicle, the engine started and he was run over by his own car. Luckily he was unhurt, but he then had to repair a dog-cart which his car had crashed into before he could finally leave! Included among the many old signs of the New Inn are several beautifully painted signs for the different bars and rooms, including the Tree Tops Wine Bar, Chapman's Emporium and Old Tap Barrel Bar (both 'Purveyors of Real Ales'), Pilgrims Brewery, Carvery & Grill Restaurant, and Grey's Coffee House. There is also a fabulous original tariff board.

PURVEYORS OF REAL ALES

NEW INN
HOTEL
TARIFF
s. d.
Passengers Superior Accommodation 7 6
Coachmen & Ostler Accommodation 3 0
Full Livery & Stabling per Horse 1 6
Horses changed, Trace Horses (pair) 2 0
~ Harness repairs undertaken ~
Josiah Chapman Inn Keeper

TREE
TOPS
WINE
BAR

NEW INN

NEW INN
CHAPMAN'S EMPORIUM

GREYS
COFFEE
HOUSE

EST. 1872
PILGRIMS BREWERY
GLOUCESTER

Prince of Wales

Station Road

With its cream and blue painted exterior, this three-storey Victorian pub has been likened to a wedding cake. It was once perfectly situated to tempt travellers from the Midland railway station (later named Eastgate station). However, the station closed in 1975 and its former site is now an ASDA supermarket. It was planned that the pub would be doubled in size in 2002 to accommodate extra business from the completion of the new £15 million GL1 leisure centre, but this never materialised, and the pub closed down that same year. It has been left boarded up and empty ever since.

The Abbey

Northgate Street

This attractive new sign suggests that the art of painting signs onto brick is not entirely extinct; it was painted when Varsity bar became the Abbey in October 2012, following a £140,000 refurbishment. The Abbey name comes from the fact that the pub's garden leads through to Gloucester Cathedral, which was once an abbey.

R. Morris, Coach Builder

Market Parade

Time has not been kind to this old sign, which is now almost unreadable. I have just about been able to identify it as that of R. Morris, a local coach builder. His business is first listed in 1847, and should the sign have been around as long as the business itself, this would make it one of the oldest in the city.

Automobile Services

Russell Street

This sign has proved somewhat mysterious as I could not find any garages, dealerships or other 'automobile services' ever listed at this address. Perhaps it was part of an advert for a business located elsewhere.

Car Parking Double Sign

Russell Street

A quirky double-painted car parking sign: 'Emergency Keep Clear' has been changed to 'Private Car Park'. The original could have been linked to the 'Automobile Services' sign above.

Dawes House Decorator

Park Road

Although quite faded now, this sign would have been eye-catching in its day, with its large, white, slab-serif lettering. F.W. Dawes House Decorator is listed as being on London Road from roughly 1902–42, but there seems to be no record of his presence here on Park Road. Perhaps this sign was simply an off-site advertisement for his services.

Bedford Street Motors

Bedford Street

This attractive hand-painted sign is just beginning to fade slightly in places, but the personal touches of the sign painter, along with the simple colours, make it stand out from many of the similar modern signs in the city. It looks like the phone number has been changed at some point to black numbers, which are less in-keeping, but the rest of the sign seems to be unchanged.

Journal and Citizen Office

St John's Lane & Southgate Street

The *Gloucester Journal*, founded by Robert Raikes Sr and William Dicey, was first published in 1722. Following the death of his father in 1758, Robert Raikes Jr took over the business and based it on Southgate Street. The timbered building is still known as Robert Raikes House and is now a pub. The *Citizen* newspaper was established by Samuel Bland in 1876. During April of that year, placards had popped up all over Gloucester, displaying a single word – CITIZEN. Nobody knew what they meant, until the mystery was solved when the *Citizen* newspaper was first published on 1 May. It was four pages long and cost half a penny. The two papers later joined forces when Thomas Henry Chance, then owner of the *Gloucester Journal*, went into partnership with Samuel Bland, and in 1879 the two papers both relocated to St John's Lane. There were originally two buildings on either side of the lane, connected by a small footbridge bearing the words 'The Citizen & Gloucester Journal', but, following a fire in 1931, the offices had to be rebuilt, after which only the left side of the lane was used. The *Citizen* remained at these offices until 2007, when they moved to Cheltenham to share a location with the *Cheltenham Echo*. This decision did not go down well – the move was condemned by the city's MP, city councillors and former staff, who held a 'wake' in protest. Led by the 'Grim Reaper', they carried a coffin from the city council offices at North Warehouse to The Cross, where a 'memorial service' was held, before a wreath was then laid outside the former *Citizen* offices. Many felt that the *Citizen* had recklessly severed its links with the Gloucester community that had been built over hundreds of years. Only a small regional office now remains in Gloucester on The Oxebode.

A.G. Meek, Shoes & Accessories

Westgate Street

The modern shopfront gives no clues to this shop's past. However, A.G. Meek has been a feature of Westgate Street for almost fifty years, and a walk down the alleyway to the side of the building reveals its shoe repair bar and some rather older signage. In fact, A.G. Meek has recently celebrated a century in business thanks to its other, older branches in Cardiff and Newport. A surprise discovery was made at the Westgate Street building in 2012, when repair work on a bricked-up fireplace uncovered a copy of the *Citizen* newspaper in the pile of coal. It was dated 1891, and had been sat there for 122 years, far outdating the existence of A.G. Meek at the premises. Who knows why the fire had never been lit?

Letterpress and Copperplate Printers

Berkeley Street

This wonderfully preserved sign proved something of a mystery for a while, as it lacks any mention of a specific company or owner name, and I was unable to find any printers ever listed on Berkeley Street. However, I believe it belonged to Thomas Birt, who is listed as a letterpress and copperplate printer on the adjacent Westgate Street in 1820, making it one of the oldest original signs that I have found in Gloucester.

Nevitt of Gloucester

Southgate Street

Lighting specialists J. & E. Nevitt were established in 1970, and have showrooms in Gloucester and Worcester. Although relatively new compared to most of the shops featured in this book, Nevitt's façade and signage are reminiscent of a much earlier twentieth-century style, with the dark wood exterior and traditional lettering harking back to a pre-chain store era.

G.A. Baker & Son

Southgate Street

Jewellers G.A. Baker started trading in 1882 from an old medieval house, but moved to this building, with its beautiful Edwardian shopfront, in 1904. The fabulously well-preserved features include gilt lettering on the signage (which would have been delicately hand-painted with gold-leaf), but even more impressive are the clock and bell-striking figures that chime on the hours and quarters. The figures (left to right) are: an Irish woman, John Bull (personifying England), Father Time, a Scotsman and a Welsh woman. The business is now run by the Mann family, who have themselves been trading in Gloucester for a

staggering 273 years and counting. Eight generations of the family have retailed on or near the city's cross since 1741. Their original shop was demolished in the early twentieth century to make way for the tram system, and they were forced to relocate to Eastgate Street, before moving to the Baker building in 1988. At one time they boasted ownership of twelve establishments, before the recession of the late 1980s forced them to reduce the number back down to a single shop. In recent years, the number of shops has increased again to five.

Criterion Hotel

Commercial Road

Criterion Hotel dates back to at least 1893 as a pub and hotel. The pub closed its doors in 1993 and the hotel followed in 2002. The building is now used for residential purposes, but still retains the hotel sign and coat of arms-style logo.

Kimbrose Hotel

Commercial Road

This three-star hotel has an attractive hand-painted sign hanging outside, with unique personal touches which make it stand out. You'll notice that the letters are shaded in red to the lower left. You might also notice that most other hand-painted signs are shaded to the lower left rather than right, and there is a very good reason for this! The letter E is the most frequently used letter in the English language, and sign painters use mainly capital letters in their work – making the capital E the most ubiquitous letter in sign-painting. A shade to the lower right on a capital E uses eight brushstrokes, whereas it takes just four strokes to shade it to the lower left – a no-brainer for sign painters looking to be as time-efficient and cost-effective as possible in their work.

The hotel has a rather less attractive sign on the other side of the building which, despite being newer, is falling apart.

Quality Furniture, Gloucester Furniture Exhibition Centre

Southgate Street

The huge signs spelling out 'Quality Furniture' on both sides of this building are difficult to miss. The large cut-out letters aligned to horizontal bars – coupled with the choice of lettering style – give the signs a bold style that may have drawn influence from the large, three-dimensional signs that were popular in twentieth-century America. I'm glad that the impressive signs have been retained, although I can't help but the think the building would look more attractive if the style of the more modern signage on ground-floor level was more sympathetically tied with the older signs. Gloucester Furniture Exhibition centre has been trading from this large Victorian warehouse since 1975. It features two floors of furniture, and has its very own Roman wall that forms part of the ground-floor showroom. The family run company was founded in 1972 and has another centre in Worcester.

Black Swan Hotel

Southgate Street

This elegant Neo-Classical building was originally named the Black Horse in 1919, renamed the Yeoman in 1970, and renamed again as the Black Swan in the 1990s. It was known for its real ales and won the Gloucester Branch of CAMRA 'Pub of the Year' in 2000. Plans to refurbish the pub interior and build a stylistically sympathetic fourteen-bedroom extension to the Grade II listed building in 2002 never materialised, and instead the Black Swan closed in 2003. The building was redeveloped for residential use, and during the development some interesting finds were made. On the front of the building, the removal of the modern signs revealed older lettering on the masonry, with the wording 'Black Swan Hotel'. There are also two fading signs on the front of the building which curiously say 'Go by Road' and 'Send by Road'. An old enamel sign saying 'Black Swan Hotel. Family and Commercial' was also discovered and can now be seen displayed in the foyer. A much older sign from the hotel's days as the Yeoman is also on display at the Gloucester Regiment's museum at the docks.

The Nelson Inn

Southgate Street

The Nelson Inn is an attractive, green glazed tiled pub. It has existed since around 1815, and has been through a few variations of the name since. It was originally named the Nelson's Head Inn, followed by the Lord Nelson Inn, before the Nelson Inn was settled on in 1847. Perhaps the changes were due to the fact that pub names inevitably get shortened by punters – this pub is invariably known as simply 'The Nelson' by local drinkers. It was owned by Brimscombe Brewery, followed by George's (of Bristol), Courage and Ushers. The façade of the building has barely changed over the years – the pub's name can still be seen in large gold letters, although the brickwork has been painted white and the original windows bearing the brewery name are long gone.

Talbot's Bottlers (Gloucester) Ltd, Wholesale Beer Bottlers

Ladybellegate Street

This building was home to Talbot Bottlers' offices, where they were based since at least 1867. The main factory was located on Commercial Road. Another property was also listed in 1959 as being at 141 Westgate Street. Their products included seltzer water, potass water, lemonade, soda water, ginger ale, magnesia water, aerated lime juice, lithia water, quinine tonic water and orange champagne – 'the finest non-alcoholic beverage ever introduced'. Talbot's mineral water was often seen advertised on the trams that once ran through the city centre. One glowing testimonial from a printed advert reads:

> Messrs Talbot & Co.,
> Gentlemen – I have evaporated down the contents of the bottles of Soda Water you sent me, and searched for lead and other metals, but without effect, so that you can rest assured of the freedom of the water from any metallic contamination.
> I am Gentlemen,
> Yours truly,
> John Horsley, Analytical Chemist
> The Laboratory, Cheltenham
> February nineteenth 1875

The company proudly claimed the 'richest award' at the Great International Health Exhibition in London, 1884. You can see one of their surviving original bottles here.

Pickfords Removers & Storers

Located at Northgate Street & Parliament Street

This sign for Pickfords Removal Company was painted twice and although the most recent version is far more prominent, both are showing through. Pickfords was based on Parliament Street from the 1930s, and also had properties on Northgate Street and Henry Road. Their name can frequently be seen on removal vehicles and scaffolding in old photographs and films of the city. Today, Pickfords is an international moving company which is said to have existed since the seventeenth century. It still has a presence in Gloucester, albeit at a different address – they are now located at the Gloucester Business Park in Brockworth.

... Good ... Complete ...

Alvin Street

Here you can see the top and bottom sections of a rather faded sign that has become very difficult to make out. I suspect it may be the combination of more than one sign overlapping. The words 'good' and 'complete' can be seen on the lower section, but that's about all. Maybe there are more clues hidden behind the modern advertising board that covers the centre of the sign.

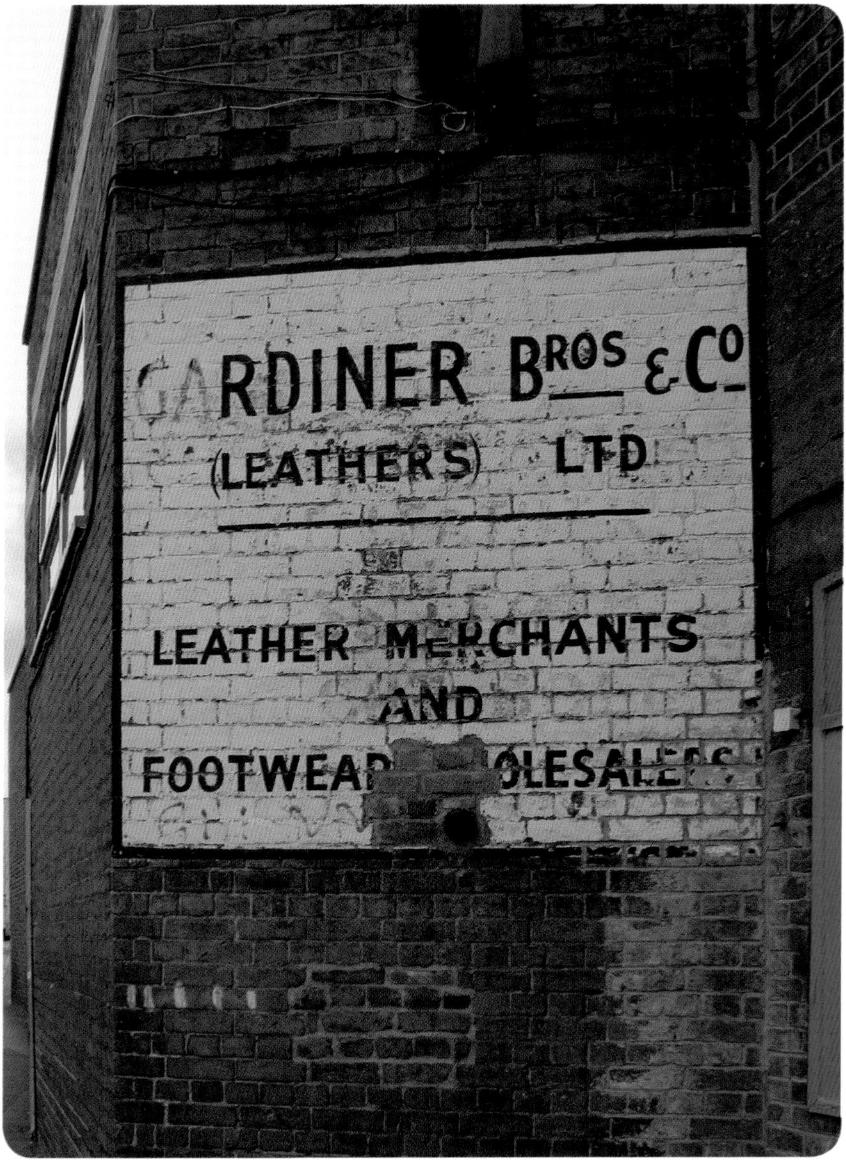

Gardiner Bros & Co. (Leathers) Ltd

Alvin Street

Established in 1860, Gardiner Bros were advertised as 'tanners and curriers'. From their shop in Alvin Street they mended and sold shoes, as well as nails, rivets, sewing needles and 'Brunner's "Excelsior" Compo for preserving machine belts, and causing them to adhere to pulleys'. They also had a tannery in Evesham. Gardiner Bros are remarkably still selling footwear, albeit no longer at this address. The international company is still based in Gloucester, but now at the Quedgeley Business Park.

Rootes Group Distributors

London Road

Despite being partially obscured by modern advertising, this sign can still be identified as saying 'Rootes Group Distributors'. It belonged to Taylor's Crypt House Motors, who were distributors for the Rootes Group in Gloucester from about 1936 until 1967. Rootes Group was an automobile manufacturer which was based in the Midlands and south of England from 1913 until 1971, when its takeover was completed by Chrysler, who later sold the company in parts to both Peugeot and Renault. Rootes Group produced several well-known British cars including the Commer, Karrier, Hillman, Humber, Singer, Sunbeam and Talbot. Vehicle carriers bearing the Rootes Group name can often be seen in old films of Gloucester city centre.

Woolworths

Eastgate Street

F.W. Woolworth & Co. opened in Gloucester in the early 1920s, and gradually expanded its presence in the city, often displacing smaller local businesses in the process, such as Blinkhorn's, which it bought out in 1953. Woolworths was one of the major casualties of the recent recession, closing its doors in Gloucester for the final time on 2 January 2009. After lying empty for over three years, the building on Eastgate Street is now occupied by Marks & Spencer. This photograph was taken in 2010, when all that remained was this shadow of where the sign had been.

Norville Opticians/Norville Optical Company

Eastgate Street/Tarrington Road/Paul Street

The Norville Optical Company began its life in 1957, based in Gloucester. Their sites included an optician's on Eastgate Street, a factory on Tarrington Road/Paul Street in Tredworth and an office on Russell Street. The Eastgate Street optician's advert on the side of the building is one of the most well-known old signs in Gloucester, and different generations can recall buying their glasses there. Despite changes to the format of telephone numbers over the years, the original sign has been left unaltered. The front of the building also features a sign with fantastic gilt lettering, although the newer sign above the door is less in-keeping.

The old works in Hatherley Road, Tredworth, were closed in 2005, and were later targeted by arsonists in February 2012. The fire gutted the derelict building which had been thought of as an eyesore by neighbours, who were forced to evacuate for around an hour during the blaze. It took almost thirty firefighters more than ten hours to battle the 60m-high flames. Although the business no longer trades as The Norville Optical Company, it still exists under the guise of its parent company, the Norville Group and its subsidiaries, which still manufacture cutting-edge optical equipment that is sold all over the world.

2

BARTON & TREDWORTH

The Corner Store

Tarrington Road/Hatherley Road

Opposite the old Norville works, the relic of a store that once stood here can be seen on the corner of what is now a residential property. It is clear that the door that once stood here has been bricked in. No doubt this corner shop made a lot of its profit from the passing trade of the Norville employees, so it is no surprise to see that it has also since gone out of business.

H. Poole Fish/Fruit/Veg/Potato Merchants

High Street

Henry 'Harry' Poole traded here from at least 1955 and would ride his bike up to the railway station at about 5 a.m. each day to collect fresh fish, which had arrived from Grimsby. This lovely old sign suggests that he could have done with a more concise phrase to describe all the things that he sold! Looking at it closely, you can also see that there are two signs here, both for H. Poole. The first reads 'Phone 2537 H Poole over 30 years Reliable People For Fish Suppers', whilst the second reads 'H Poole Fish Fruit Vegetable Salesman Potato Merchant. All Kinds of Fruit Bought. All Fish Received From Coast ????' – the last word can't quite be made out.

Smith & Choyce Ltd

Barton Street

Smith & Choyce Joinery have been operating from Barton Street for around eighty years. The business is still family run, with current managing director Martin Choyce the fourth generation to run the business. The company now also lets out industrial units to a diverse selection of tenants, ranging from a pole-dancing school to nuclear engineering specialists.

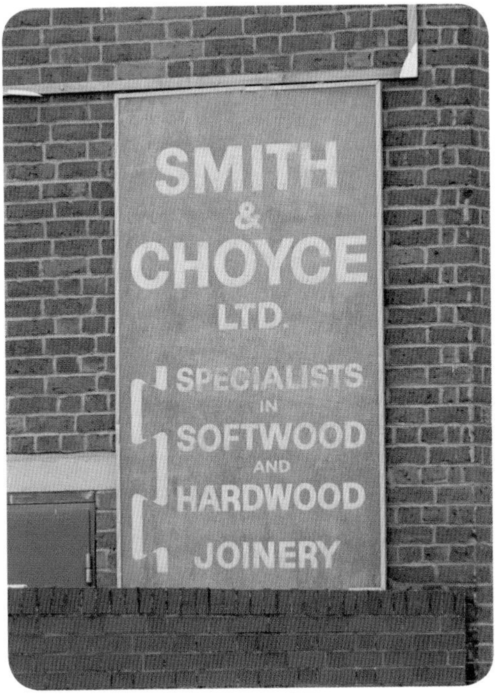

More News Daily

Barton Street

Although the elements have caused this Sunday Telegraph advert to become very rusty, it is still quite clear to read and remains an interesting feature outside Norat's Newsagents.

Nestlé

Dynevor Street

Everyone knows the Nestlé brand, and this large painted advert must have been quite a sight in its day. It is rather faded these days, but 'Nestle's Milk Richest in Cream' can still be made out quite easily. These two printed adverts from around 1900 boast the same tagline, and a stark warning to cats everywhere that skim milk will leave you emaciated, whereas Nestlé milk is essential for a silky coat and sound 'limb and brain'. It seems that the inclusion, or lack of, accent on the second E of Nestlé varied from advert to advert.

Morses Homemade Bread

Dynevor Street

Alongside the Nestlé sign, this large advert reads 'To be well fed, eat & enjoy Morses homemade bread, sold here.' Morse was one of two bakeries in the Tredworth area in the 1940s, the other being Sparkes.

Sparkes Bakery

Ryecroft Street

Sparkes bakery began life in 1850, but it wasn't until 1961 that they moved to Gloucester. They originally had several bakery sites in Ryecroft Street before centralising the business at No. 63. The business closed in August 1985, but is remembered fondly for its dripping cakes and baked goods, including their hot cross buns, which were produced in their hundreds for schools and events in the local area. At times, the queue of customers would run out the door and down the street, which would be blocked up with cars as people rushed to get their bread and cakes in the mornings! This meant a cruel work schedule for the bakers, who would be up at 5 a.m. to stoke the ovens, and would often work until about 9 p.m., six days a week. The business was also a general grocery, selling other products such as sweets and tobacco. As you can see, both the bakery's own wonderfully characterful hand-painted sign and a stylish Hovis advertisement survive.

SPARKES
Estd 1850
BAKERY

HOVIS

Road Ra …

Charles Street/Barton Street

Unfortunately a large portion of this old painted sign has been covered up by modern billboards, however, a few words can be made out, and what looks like the image of a chequered flag. Although these clues are tantalising, it is not clear what business the advert was for.

• • •

Victory Road/Tredworth Road

This mysterious sign can be seen on a house on Tredworth Road, although it has become impossible to decipher.

Ye Olde Robin Hood Inn

Hopewell Street

The splendid frontage of this pub features green glazed tiles and a secondary sign, which reads 'Stroud Brewery Ales & Stout'; it also once had impressive etched Stroud Brewery windows. It is unclear why the Robin Hood name was chosen, as Gloucester has no obvious connection to the heroic outlaw. However it was not alone – it outlasted another nineteenth-century pub of the same name which existed on Bristol Road. The Hopewell Street pub has existed since at least 1872, when it was first recorded, although it was rebuilt in 1908 by the Stroud Brewery, who spent a remarkable amount of money on the façade of what is no more than a small local pub. It sadly closed in November 1977, whilst under Whitbread ownership, and it was only after the Whitbread sign was removed that the original Stroud Brewery features were rediscovered. This listed building is now a cultural centre for the Gloucester Muslim Welfare Association.

The Vauxhall Inn

Barton Street

Originally a Victorian pub, this building is an eye-catching sight on Barton Street. Built in the Arts and Crafts style, with glazed polychromatic tiles surrounding the ground-floor exterior, as well as swan-neck pediments and various other elaborate details, the building is certainly extravagant. It was built in 1876 by Mitchells & Butlers, and has been said to be named after Vauxhall Pleasure Gardens in London. The area around the inn did indeed once feature an attached pleasure garden (Blenheim Gardens) and a private zoo! It closed in 2008 and became Barton Street's first supermarket, but the exterior decoration has been thoughtfully preserved – it is definitely more lavish than your typical supermarket!

Princes Plume

Barton Street

The Princes Plume was a pub built in 1905. It closed in 1990, and the building has since been home to a bicycle shop, and is now a tile and hardware store with residential flats above. Although the raised lettering saying 'celebrated fine ales & stout' is still visible, the Princes Plume name has been covered by the shop's sign.

St James Club

Barton Street

St James Club was originally founded in 1901 as a working men's club. The word 'men's' was dropped from the name in 2004 and the members' club is today a popular location for family friendly community gatherings in the Barton and Tredworth area. I can't be certain, but looking at the spacing of the signs, I suspect that 'working' and 'men's' originally sat on the central section of the building, and were simply removed when the name was changed.

Phitform Boots

Barton Street/Stratton Road

This excellent old sign has become rather faded, and it looks as if there are now elements of two different over-painted signs showing through. At least one of the signs seems to have been an advertisement for shoes. These words can still be made out: 'Our Shoes … Special … Brands … Graceful & Durable. The … Phitform Boots, Reg, For Men, 8/11-10 … 16/6, Sold … Wear Guaranteed.' There are clearly some words missing, but you can still get the general idea they were trying to convey! The sign could have belonged to either

of two shoe shops that were based here. F.J.H. Cartwright boot and shoe depot was listed here in 1906, but by 1916 the premises were occupied by J.N. Brown & Co. boot and shoe depot. It's not clear whether the original business changed hands (and name) or whether these were completely separate businesses.

The Gloucester Furnishing Company

Barton Street

Opportunistically squeezed between the windows is this sign for The Gloucester Furnishing Company, who traded here from about 1906 to 1920. You can see how the sign painter has used condensed lettering to make the lower part of the sign as large as possible in the narrow space. In the age of computer fonts, we would call these kind of simple letters sans-serif, but to the traditional sign painter these are known as Modern Egyptian letters.

Payne's T.V.

Painswick Road

This television shop has been derelict for several years now. Customers no doubt shifted elsewhere due to the presence of electronic retail giants in the city, as well as the rise of internet shopping.

Gloucester Irish Club

Horton Road

As you can see, this fading painted sign clearly says 'The GLOUCESTER …' – but the remainder of the sign is covered up on the right-hand side of the building by the newer signage. You might think this was the original Gloucester Irish Club sign, but it is said that it was in fact that of the Gloucester Pin Manufacturing Company, who used the premises as a factory from roughly 1914 to 1927. By 1945 the building was owned by the British Institute of Herbal Remedies of which G.R. Lane MA was principal. This later went on to be known as G.R. Lane, pharmaceutical remedies, and then Lanes Health, manufacturers of Olbas Oil. The company was based here until 1972. The Gloucester Irish Club was formed by Irish exiles in 1964 to provide Gloucester's growing Irish community with a focal point for cultural and social activities. The club was originally located on Station Road but moved to Horton Road in 1975. In the 1960s and '70s the club's membership was huge, but the upturn in the Irish economy in the 1990s saw many of Gloucester's Irish residents return to their home country to work. The club is still very active, boasting Irish dancing and music, and reputedly the cheapest Guinness in town! The gates to the car park also feature some nice touches, with shamrocks on the railings and gold harps atop the corners.

GLOU

Williams & James Engineers, Air Compressors/Reducing Valves

Chequers Bridge (over Barton Street)

Founded in 1915, Williams & James made hydraulic and pneumatic machinery for the motor car industry, employing as many as 250 people in the early 1960s. They were eventually bought out by Hamworthy Belliss & Morcom Ltd in 1987.

3

DOCKS

North Warehouse

The signs bearing the warehouse names have all been retouched and repainted at various points in time to maintain them, and some have replaced older signs bearing company names, but they retain their original style. North Warehouse was the first warehouse to be built at Gloucester Docks, and served as a model for the others that followed. It was completed in 1827 by the Canal Company whilst construction of the canal itself was being completed, and would serve as a place to store cargo. Many different merchants used the warehouse, importing wheat, barley, oats, wines and spirits from Ireland and Europe. During the twentieth century the building was occupied by Priday Metford & Co., who also ran the nearby City Flour Mills. They moved out in 1962 and the condition of the building began to deteriorate. By the late 1970s the building was in a state of some disrepair, and despite being listed as being of Special Architectural and Historic Interest, British Waterways applied for listed building consent for demolition, arguing that their responsibility was to run the canals, not to restore uneconomic buildings. Fortunately they were not granted consent, and the building survived. It was bought by the City Council for just £1, for use as their main offices. Much restoration work was needed – most of the roof had to be replaced, along with some rotten woodwork, but wherever possible the original timbers were kept intact. The work was finished in July 1986, proving that the warehouses could be adapted for modern uses whilst retaining their original features. This example was something of a trigger for the redevelopment of the docks, which has been ongoing for the last thirty years or so.

Victoria Warehouse

Victoria Warehouse was built in 1849 for the merchant William Partridge and was originally known as Mr Partridge's Warehouse. However, when both Albert and Britannia Warehouses were also built for him, it became necessary to give them each a distinctive name. As a result they were named patriotically after queen, king and country. Victoria Warehouse was initially rented to Wait James & Co., before they moved to Llanthony Warehouse in 1873. The building was later used by Cadle & Co., the Severn Ports Warehousing Co. and S.W. Lane, corn merchants. When Sidney Lane went bankrupt in 1900, Turner Nott & Co., corn merchants, took over and occupied the premises until 1926. Following this, the building stood empty for a decade before being leased to builders' merchants Sessions and Sons until 1962. Priday Metford & Co. then used the warehouse for storing and bagging flour from their nearby City Flour Mills until 1989. Although it is now very difficult to make out, and it looks like there may be more than one painted sign showing through, I believe that the faded sign beneath the Victoria Warehouse Lane is that of S.W. Lane Round & Co.

Albert Warehouse

Albert Warehouse was built in 1851 and also owned by William Partridge. The building was initially rented by the corn merchants W.C. Lucy & Co., but was taken over by James Reynolds, the owner of milling company J. Reynolds & Co., in 1869. They converted the building into a flour mill with a boiler and engine house built to the south. The mill was closed in 1977 and the ancillary buildings demolished. From 1984, Albert Warehouse housed the fantastic Robert Opie Museum of Advertising and Packaging, a vast collection of old packaging, advertising and branding collected over the years. I was lucky enough to visit it myself, and thoroughly enjoyed being immersed in the rich visual history. Unfortunately the museum closed in October 2001, and Robert Opie's collection has since been relocated to the Museum of Brands, Packaging and Advertising in Notting Hill, London, to try to attract a greater footfall and range of visitors.

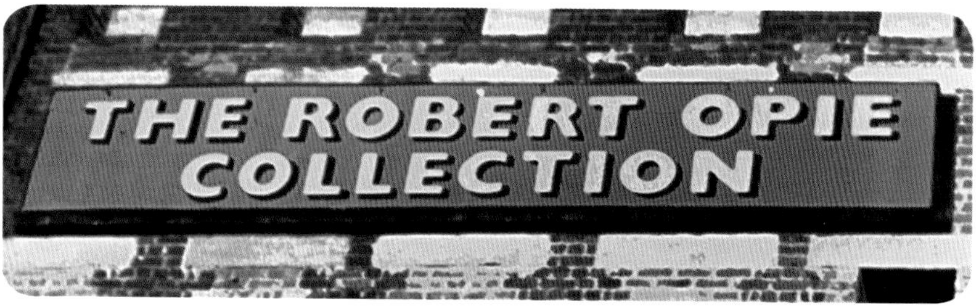

Britannia Warehouse

Built in 1861, and again owned by William Partridge, Britannia Warehouse was first rented to the corn merchants H. Adams & Co. before being leased to the warehouseman G.T. Beard, who managed several of the warehouses, storing grain for a number of merchants who did not have their own premises. From the 1930s onwards the building was no longer used to store grain, and was subsequently occupied by various companies such as millwrights W.S. Barron & Son, exhibition display builders Priestly Studios, Cotswold Typesetting and removal firm Loader & Munckton. In 1987 the warehouse was completely gutted by fire, which, after much debate, led to it being demolished and rebuilt using many of the original bricks.

Lock Warehouse

Named simply due to its position next to the lock, this warehouse was built in 1834 for corn merchants J. & C. Sturge. It was originally constructed with the ground floor raised on cast-iron columns a few feet above the ground, although it was later decided that the floors were not adequately supported when loaded with heavy sacks of corn, and was eventually lowered to ground level. J. & C. Sturge occupied the building until the early 1880s, when it was subsequently used by corn merchants Spillers & Co. (later known as Spillers & Bakers), sack-hire company Gospill Brown & Sons, and builders' merchants Jennings, Guildings & Co., before being converted into a furniture restoration workshop in 1979. In 2010 the warehouse became the Arts & Crafts Centre, and the building has since been converted into residential apartments.

R.F. Hamblin (Joinery) Ltd

Founded in 1973, R.F. Hamblin was a joinery and manufacturing company specialising in cork and straw items as well as plaiting material. The company closed down in 1994, although according to business records it seems it was restored for a brief spell in 2010 before being dissolved again in 2011. There are some interesting signs remaining around the building, including an extremely narrow fire exit – I can't imagine it would be deemed safe today.

Reynolds Warehouse

Reynolds Warehouse has also been known as Sturge's Warehouse at times, as it was built in 1840 for the corn merchants J. & C. Sturge. It was also used by corn merchants S.W. Lane, G.T. Beard, and later its namesake, J. Reynolds & Co. On the back of the warehouse you can still make out a fading sign spelling out 'S.W. Lane Round & Co.' It has more recently been converted into residential flats.

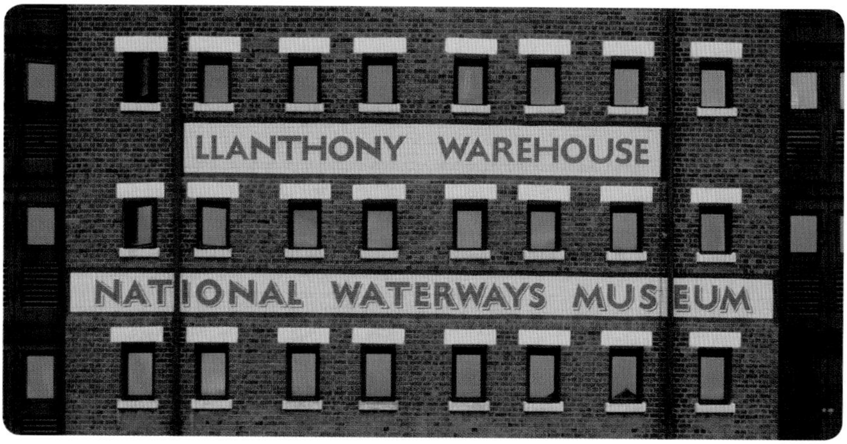

Llanthony Warehouse, (Gloucester Waterways Museum)

Built in 1873, Llanthony Warehouse was originally owned by Wait James & Co., corn merchants, and was also used by Western trading Co., builders' merchants. You can still see part of Wait James & Co.'s faded old sign above the Llanthony Warehouse sign. The period spanning from post-war to the 1970s saw reckless architectural destruction en masse, as modernist new approaches to city planning led to historical buildings being demolished to make way for more functional and easily maintainable buildings, and Gloucester was no exception. In 1972 the British Waterways Board tried to demolish Llanthony Warehouse to make way for modern developments, but were thankfully denied permission. The original building still stands and now houses the Gloucester Waterways Museum (formerly known as the National Waterways Museum), which was opened by Prince Charles in 1988, after a £3.2 million conversion.

Powell Lane Manufacturing Company

Severn Road

Although Powell Lane may sound like a street name, it was actually a combination of the surnames of Messrs Powell and Lane. They were paper merchants in the early twentieth century, and this is where their offices were based. There are some interesting adverts

painted on the side of the building. I can just about make out the words 'M. Hay Colliery Agent' and 'House & Steam Com' on the lower left sign. The top sign appears to be that of Powell Lane Manufacturing Company, and it looks like there could also be a third, different sign painted over, but too much of it is obscured by the (nicely hand-painted) modern sign for the antiques centre.

Securicor Ltd

This long-abandoned shipping container spotted at the docks belonged to Securicor (security services), who once had premises on London Road. The company started life in London in 1936 as 'Nightwatch Services' – a team of bike-riding guards in police uniform. They changed their name to 'Security Corps' in 1951, and then Securicor in 1953.

Biddle Warehouse

Originally owned by John Biddle, a miller from Stroud, this warehouse has also been used by John Weston & Co., corn merchants, as well as the Severn & Canal Carrying Co. This warehouse is unusual compared to the others in that it has larger windows with segmental heads; this appears to have been a stylistic choice borrowed by the architect from the cloth mills of Stroud, where he was from. Today the building is used for both residential and retail purposes.

Herbert Warehouse

Built in 1846 and originally owned by the solicitor Samuel Herbert, this warehouse was principally used by J. & C. Sturge, corn merchants, and T. Robinson & Co., also corn merchants. The existing building is a 1988 rebuild of the nineteenth-century warehouse, which fits almost seamlessly among the older warehouses.

Kimberley Warehouse

Built in 1846 and originally owned by Humphrey Brown, this warehouse was mainly used by J.P. Kimberley, corn merchants, and G.T. Beard, warehouseman. The building now houses City Council offices as well as Dr Foster's pub and restaurant.

Phillpotts Warehouse

This warehouse was built in 1846 and named after its original owner A.H. Phillpotts, who used it for his corn merchant company Phillpotts & Co. The building now houses Edinburgh Woollen Mill and City Council offices.

Shipton Warehouse

Shipton Warehouse was built in 1833 and was originally owned by the timber merchant J.M Shipton. It was also used by Bretherton & Pitchford, corn merchants, S.W. Lane, corn merchant, and the Severn and Canal Carrying Co. Today the building houses residential apartments.

Alexandra Warehouse

Alexandra Warehouse was built in 1870 for the corn merchants J.E. & S.H. Fox. In 1875 it was badly damaged by a fire that started in the eaves – above the limited reach of the primitive fire services of the time. However, the building was soon rebuilt, and continued to be occupied by the Fox family and their various partners until around 1925.

British Waterways

British Waterways was founded in 1962, and was responsible for caring for the 2,200-mile long network of canals and rivers in Britain. They oversaw the cessation of most commercial transportation via canals in the early 1960s, reasons for which included the Clean Air Act 1956, the building of the first motorways and the particularly harsh winter of 1962, in which many of the canals were frozen solid. Today the remaining canals are used mainly for leisure purposes.

British Waterways' charitable division, The Waterways Trust, established the National Waterways Museum – of which there are three – at Gloucester Docks, Stoke Bruerne and Ellesmere Port. British Waterways ceased to exist in England and Wales as of 2 July 2012, and was replaced by the Canal & River Trust, although it still continues as a legal entity in Scotland, albeit under the trading name 'Scottish Canals'. The museum at Llanthony Warehouse is now known as the Gloucester Waterways Museum.

Vinings Warehouse

Built in 1840 and originally owned by C.J. Vining, this warehouse was mainly used by his company Vining & Rea, corn merchants, as well as J. Edwards & Co., corn merchants, and J. Reynolds & Co., millers. There is a small building extending from the warehouse which sports a fading Reynolds sign. The Vinings restaurant is a more recent addition, serving a selection of pan-Asian cuisine.

Tiger Masthead

This terrific figurehead is surprisingly easy to miss, tucked round a corner atop a shipping container. Whether it waits to adorn a ship once again or whether it has simply been rescued by an admirer is unclear.

G. & W.E. Downing Maltsters

Merchants Road

George and William E. Downing were in fact from Smethwick in the West Midlands, but they opened their first malthouse in Gloucester in 1876 before expanding to a second in 1895. The lack of any windows on the upper floors of this particular building gave them plenty of space to advertise, as you can see! This huge sign was actually painted twice and elements of both versions show through today, making it rather confusing to read. The first version was painted with the names of towns and cities in large letters, but as the business expanded it became necessary to list more locations and so the sign was repainted with smaller lettering. There is also some expertly engraved signage above the door for G. & W.E. Downing's offices. As you will notice, the building was later occupied by West Midland Farmers Association, who had also acquired Island Mills in lower Westgate Street in around 1920, and British Oil & Cake Mills' property at Baker's Quay in 1955. They expanded further in the 1970s before buying G. & W.E. Downing's disused malthouses in 1983 for grain storage. The future of the buildings remains uncertain at this time; the listed buildings are in a bad state of repair and will require substantial investment to make them useable again.

MALTSTERS
BRANCH
SMETHWICK
BIRMINGHAM
WEST BROMWICH
WEDNESBURY
WALSALL

ABM

Merchants Road

This connecting bridge attached to the G. & W.E. Downing malthouses is painted with the letters ABM, which stood for Associated British Maltsters. Founded in 1805, ABM was an amalgamation of several different companies which kept their own names, but traded under the ABM umbrella group. Samuel Thompson & Sons had joined ABM in 1928, before taking over G. & W.E. Downing in 1931. Although Thompson had opted to retain the G. & W.E. Downing name for Gloucester-based operations, ABM was taken over by Australian company Dalgety in 1972, who replaced the Downing name with ABM; it was around this time that this sign would have appeared. They then closed the Gloucester malthouses in 1980 following the opening of a new plant at Wallingford. The site on Merchants Road was then sold to the West Midland Farmers Association.

West Midland Farmers Association

This dilapidated building has been empty and up for sale for some time, as a buyer willing to invest in redeveloping the site has yet to be found. It used to belong to the West Midland Farmers Association, which was an agricultural co-operative formed in 1902 under the name Beckford Farmers. It amalgamated with Winchcombe, Toddington and Cotswold Farmers Association in 1909 and took

on the WMF name. Their head office was established on Westgate Street in 1919, and a store was added at the same location in 1937. At their peak they had 5,384 members and 383 employees. In 1999, WMF merged with Midland Shires Farmers to form Countrywide Farmers, which still trades throughout the UK today.

4

BRISTOL ROAD AREA

Sunlight Soap Advert

Bristol Road

Launched in 1885, Sunlight was the world's first packaged, branded laundry soap. It is still sold all over the world today, and many of these antique adverts for the brand can still be found all over the country. The 'Hot & Cold Takeaway' sign is an unrelated, more recent addition. This beautiful print advert claims guaranteed purity and even offers a £1,000 reward to anyone who can prove that the soap contains 'any form of adulteration whatsoever'.

Pine …

Bristol Road/Hartington Road

This is a frustrating one. Although the lettering is still quite clear, too much of this interesting sign has been covered up by modern advertising to identify it – the word 'Pine' is the only clue. Maybe one day the rest of it will be revealed again.

Moreland's Match Factory

Bristol Road

Moreland's Match Company enjoyed many decades of making matches in Gloucester, beginning in 1867, when Samuel John Moreland, a timber merchant from Stroud, expanded his company to include a match making factory. The company is in fact even older than this, existing originally as a saw mill since 1850. The factory thrived due to its close proximity to the docks and canal, which made importing raw materials and exporting matches extremely efficient. Moreland's actually produced forty different brands, but it has become almost synonymous with its most well-known brand, England's Glory, which was adopted in 1891. At the height of its success, the factory produced a remarkable 50 million matches per day. Moreland's prided themselves on using British workers and encouraging customers to buy more British goods. One advert showed a boxer wearing Union Jack shorts and punching a (presumably foreign) competitor as they fought on a ring made of England's Glory matchboxes. The tagline read 'Strike out foreign competition by buying England's Glory Matches'. The plant was unfortunately closed in 1976, due to a number of complex reasons, including the ageing premises and accusations that they were illegally importing matches from Sweden. The sign that remains was erected in 1954 and is one of the most eye-catching in Gloucester, with its large, crossed, flaming matches and England's Glory matchbox. It is practically unchanged since the company's closure. The building is now used as a trading estate including offices and storage.

ENGLAND'S
MORELAND
GLOUCESTER
GLORY
STUDIOS - STORAGE
www.bizspace.co.uk
CARPETS
A2B TAXIS
24/7
MORELAND'S
TRADING ESTATE
Meeting Rooms
THE FURNITURE WAREHOUSE
3 PIECE
SUITES
FROM £399
THE FURNITURE WAREHOUSE
NOW OPEN
SOFAS, BEDS
MATTRESSES
&
LOTS MORE
01452 223 285
THE FURNITURE WAREHOUSE
COMPLETE
BEDS
DOUBLE £99
SINGLE £69

... ng

Seymour Road

I managed to photograph the very last remnants of this peeling old sign, just days before it was stripped away as part of repair work on the badly subsiding building. Sadly, it is not possible to identify it, as only two letters were still visible.

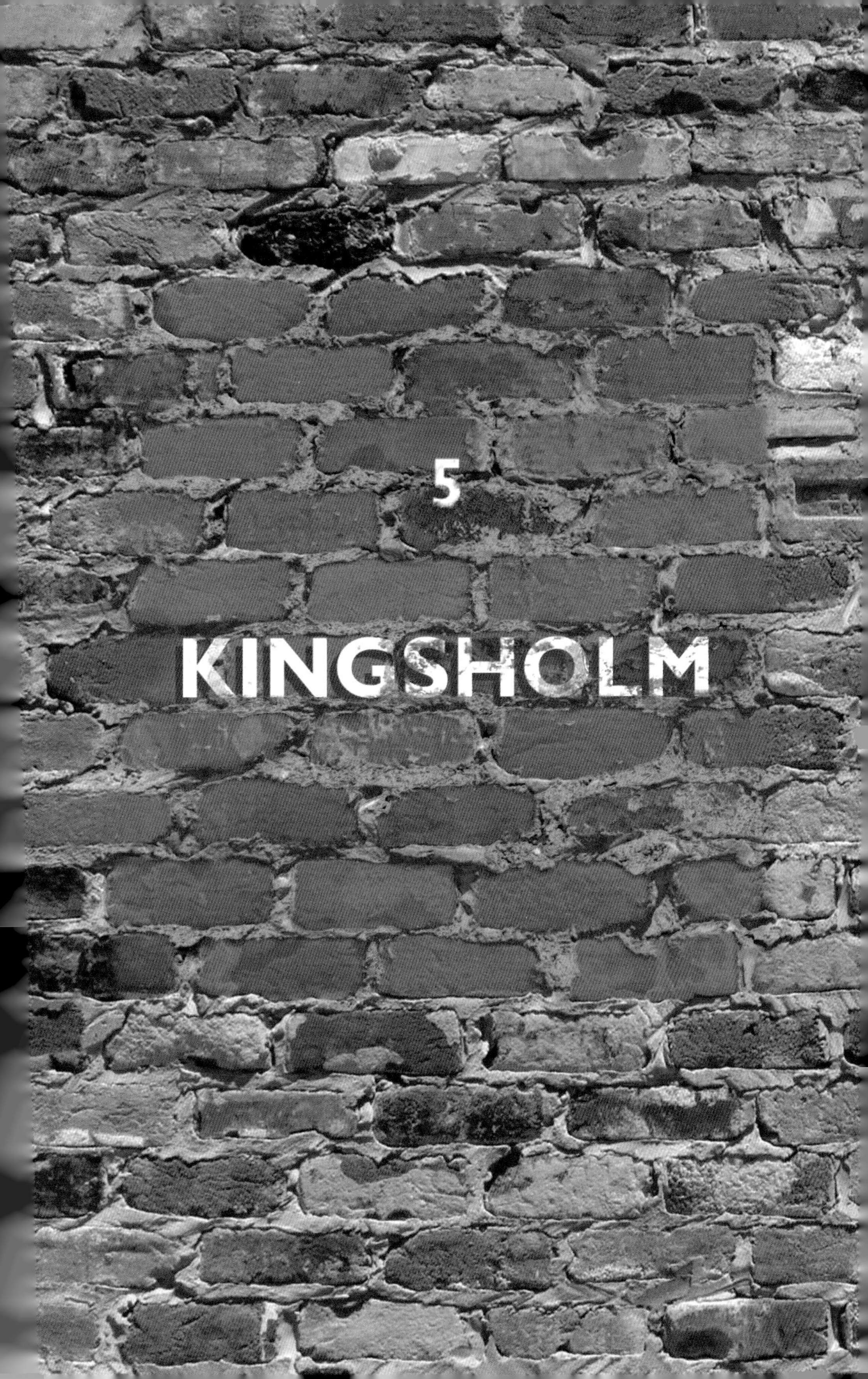

5

KINGSHOLM

The Kingsholm Inn

Kingsholm Road

Located across the road from the stadium, The Kingsholm Inn is a favourite of Gloucester's passionate rugby fans, who can be seen spilling out onto the street in front of the pub on match days. The pub has been around since at least 1847.

The White Hart

Kingsholm Road

The White Hart is another popular haunt of Gloucester rugby fans. The remnants of a faded circular sign on the side of the building can be made out to read 'Ind Coope & Co, Burton on Trent' – a brewery that was actually founded in Romford, Essex, in 1708, but opened a brewery in Burton-on-Trent in 1856. It enjoyed an extremely lengthy existence before closing in 1992.

Cooper Cowen

Kingsholm Road

This rather retro sign can be seen near the rugby stadium advertising Cooper Cowen second-hand cars.

St Mark's Church Institute

Sweetbriar Street

St Mark's Church was based in Kingsholm from 1847 to 2006. It appears that they also used this building for various purposes.

6

OTHER

Gloucester Co-operative and Industrial Society

Various Locations

The Gloucester Co-op was a formidable presence, with more than twenty branches across the county. Their numbering has become somewhat confusing over the years – No. 2 branch, built on Alvin Street in 1885 as a shop and warehouse, was in fact the eighth branch opened; No. 4 branch pictured on Stroud Road is not the original building … it is, however, over a century old. The original building was replaced by this much grander establishment after the Gloucester Co-op's golden jubilee in 1910. You can also see Branch No. 23 on Finlay Road, as well as a 1909 photograph of the Gloucester Co-op's first steam wagon parked outside one of their buildings. The body of the wagon features two different slogans – 'unity is strength' and 'each for all, all for each'.

CO-OPERATIVE
SOCIETY
LIMITED

BRANCH No2 1885

USTRIAL SOCIET
BRANCHES AT
GLOUCESTER
UNITY
IS
STRENGTH
EACH FOR ALL
ALL FOR EACH

Boselli's Ice Cream

Priory Road

Boselli's is one of the most well-known old signs in Gloucester. The business was originally owned by John Kilyan and takes its name from his wife's maiden name. The company was taken over by Len Tomalin in 1973, but closed down in 1989.

Ferodo Disc Brake Pads

Barnwood Road

This advert for Ferodo Disc Brake Pads can be seen on the railway bridge that crosses over Barnwood Road in Longlevens. Ferodo first started making brakes for horse-drawn carts in 1897, and has since supplied brakes for two land speed world record attempts: in 1926 John Godfrey Parry-Thomas set the record at 169mph, and in 1963 Donald Campbell achieved a new record of 403.1mph in the Bluebird-Proteus CN7. The brand is still around today and is now owned by Federal-Mogul. It employs over 45,000 employees in thirty-four different countries.

Oasis Car Wash

Eastern Avenue

The Oasis Car Wash is a relatively modern example of painted signage. These eye-catching signs are just beginning to fade slightly, but still make the car wash far more unique and appealing than others with cheap, mass-produced signage.

Turtle
Wax

CAR WASH
&
EXPRESS
VALET
CENTRE

BIBLIOGRAPHY

Trade Directories

Kelly's Trade Directories of Gloucester
Hunt & Co. Trade Directories of Gloucester
The Gloucestershire Directory (1820) by R. Gell & T. Bradshaw

Books

Conway-Jones, H., *A Guide to Gloucester Docks* (Gloucester: Alan Sutton Publishing, 1988)
Conway-Jones, H., *Gloucester Docks: An Illustrated History* (Gloucester: Alan Sutton Publishing/Gloucestershire County Library, 1984)
Hudson, J., *A Century of Gloucester* (Stroud: Alan Sutton Publishing, 2001)
Kirby, D., *Gloucester Then & Now* (Stroud: The History Press, 2012)
Kirby, D., *The Story of Gloucester* (Stroud: Alan Sutton Publishing, 2007)
Kirby, D., *The Story of Gloucester's Pubs* (Stroud: The History Press, 2010)
Levine, F. & Macon, S., *Sign Painters* (New York: Princeton Architectural Press, 2013)
Matthews, E.C., *How to Paint Signs and Sho' Cards* (New York: J.S. Ogilvie Publishing Company, 1920)
Moss, P., *Historic Gloucester*, 2nd Edition (Stroud: Nonsuch Publishing, 1995)
Opie, R., *Remember When*, 2nd Edition (London: Bounty Books, 2006)
Voyce, J., *The City of Gloucester* (Stroud: The Chalford Publishing Company, 1995)

Websites

www.bartonandtredworth.org.uk
www.cinematopia.co.uk
www.gloucesterdocks.me.uk
www.gloucestershirepubs.co.uk
www.livinggloucester.co.uk
www.punchline-gloucester.co.uk
www.thisisgloucestershire.co.uk